MOON OF MANY NAMES

a year of poems

By Karen Admussen

Illustrated by Selena Harris

Dedicated to my Moon Sisters

CONTENTS

JANUARY: Moondown 2

FEBRUARY: Anticipation 4

MARCH: Haiku 7

APRIL: Haiku 9

MAY: Feliz Paseos Park 10

JUNE: Hot Summer Evening 12

JULY: Haiku 15

AUGUST: Moon When All Things Ripen 16

SEPTEMBER: Sing Me a Song 18

OCTOBER: Under the Harvest Moon 20

BLUE MOON: Once in a Blue Moon 22

NOVEMBER: Beaver Moon 24

DECEMBER: Winter Warmth 26

EPILOGUE 29

PROLOGUE

Prior to moving to Arizona, I only had a few specific memories of the moon. The first one I remember is from a spring break biking trip to Missouri my senior year in college. One day my friends and I had miscalculated distances, and we ended up biking into the night to reach our campground. Under the light of the full moon that night, we had no problems seeing the road. I recall it was the first time I understood moon shadows. The lyrics from the chorus of *Moonshadow* by Cat Stevens kept repeating over and over in my mind as I pedaled.

After my college graduation, I had the crazy idea to bike back to Green Bay, Wisconsin from St. Peter, Minnesota with my dad. Like my previous bike trip, I had failed to plan well, and after packing up my dorm room, we started late on our first leg of the journey. My dad and I biked 40 miles on the Sakatah Singing Hills Trail to meet my mom at a hotel in Faribault, Minnesota. En route the sky darkened, and we finished our bike ride by the light of the full moon illuminating the trail.

Many years later my husband and I were living in Rochester, Minnesota with our two-year-old son. One night the full moon was framed perfectly in our family room window next to the fireplace. I pointed to the bright white orb filling the window and taught my son the word *moon*. I'll never forget his excitement at seeing that full moon.

My current fascination with the moon, particularly the full moon, began the first night I arrived in Tucson, Arizona. My daughter and I had just driven three long days from Chicago. We picked up the keys to our new townhouse from the realtor, bought dinner, and unpacked the car. At bedtime I realized my air mattress had a leak. It was 8 PM, and I was exhausted, but we climbed back in the car once again and drove to Target to buy a new air mattress. When we came outside, the sky was dark but gifted us a full moon directly over the peak of Pusch Ridge.

Not long after moving to Tucson, I discovered Pima County Park and Recreation hosted Full Moon Wanders at various county parks. A naturalist would lead a short, guided walk while talking about the moon, stars, and wildlife. I learned different cultures had names for each month's full moon. That first Full Moon Wander inspired me to write poems about each full moon, including a blue moon (an additional moon in a season), and explore the different names people around the world have used for each one.

JANUARY

Moondown

Waking up before sunrise
I glance out the window
a full orange moon
greets me in the west

    January's Wolf Moon
    dominating the sky
    lowers for the morning
    a moondown, a moonset

        In dawn's partial light
        the orb slowly descends
        beyond the horizon
        beside Dove Mountain

            No fanfare of wolves howling
            or brass horns blowing
            just a silent farewell
            as the night ends

                And a new day begins

FEBRUARY

Anticipation

One cold winter evening
I drive to the foothills
of the Santa Catalinas

to witness the rising
of February's Snow Moon
over Agua Caliente hill

Palm trees encircle warm water ponds
formed by a trickle of tepid water
from Agua Caliente spring

Two great horned owls
Whoowhoo from their nests
in the palm fronds

The sun begins to wane
as grackles and red-wing blackbirds
chatter in the cattails
overtaking the pond

The sky dissolves
from amber to gray
coyotes yap in the distance

Ducks swim silently
barely visible in the twilight
under palm tree shadows

With hat pulled low,
hands stuffed deep in my pockets,
I shuffle to stay warm

FEBRUARY (cont'd)

My eyes stare eastward
for the moon's debut
Stars and planets emerge
Orion and reddish-tinged Mars
appear against a black backdrop

How long will I stand
gazing up at the sky
shivering?

One illuminated cloud
foreshadows
the light to come

Finally the Supermoon
peeks over the hill
then quickly reveals
its entire splendor
of bright white light
and contoured craters

I wanted to indulge
the fullness of the moon,
the fullness of my heart

But the bitter wind
drives me back to my car
under moonlight shadows

I open the moonroof
and follow the night light,
content to let the moon's magnetic pull
draw me home as it does the tides

MARCH

March's full Worm Moon
crawls over mountain peaks
worming through moist clouds

APRIL

April's full Pink Moon
reflects blushing flowers
sunset's pastel glow

MAY

Feliz Paseos Park

A Full Moon Wander
under the May Flower Moon
elf owls chattering

Scorpions scattering
a herd of deer gathering
an enchanted night

JUNE

Hot Summer Evening

The pool beckons
warm, bath-like water soothes
no sunscreen needed

As the sun lowers
just before it disappears
mountains glow pink

Light fades to soft dusk
June Strawberry Moon rises
over rocky peaks

A planet appears
black bats fly erratically
diving for insects

Night brings cooler air
full moon shadows guide me home
under starry sky

JULY

July Thunder Moon
echoes through stony canyons,
reigns over mountains

Moon When All Things Ripen

on a hot, cloudy night
before the moon rose
I went to sleep
so I could rise early
and swim in my designated
COVID 19-free lane
causing me to miss
August's full moon

I never saw the moon
named for the month
when all things ripen:
tomatoes, blueberries
bursting with juices
wheat and barley
waving golden stalks

this year's moon
ripe for missed opportunities
like other important events
I could not attend this year:
weddings, vacations
reunions, graduations

I never saw the moon
also named for ease
in catching fish
especially sturgeon
who stir up mud and silt
in the Great Lakes
clouding the water
clouding the sky

Sing Me a Song

Sing me a song
Moon of many names

Sing me a song
A song of harvest:
      corn in the Northeast
            black cherries in Montana
                  nuts in the southern woodlands
                        mulberries in the Southeast

Sing me a song
A song of change:
      Minnesota leaves turn golden
            calves on the prairie grow thicker hair
                  Arizona nights wax slightly cooler

Sing me a song
A song of hunting:
      Inuits harpoon whales
            and seals for winter survival

Sing me a song
A song of celebration:
      birthdays
            anniversaries
                and new wine

Sing me a song
A song of death:
      the end of summer

OCTOBER

Under the Harvest Moon

Farmers reap corn
for cattle fodder
driving tractors
down row after row
through field after field
filling truck after truck

Under the Kindly Moon
far across the world
Chinese plant winter wheat
glad for a dusting of snow
which moistens the ground
and helps the plants grow

The Harvest Moon allows us to
accumulate, acquire, amass,
collect, gather, get,
pile up, reap, stash,
store, stow, stockpile
and take in . . .

While the Kindly Moon
comes in silence
arriving each October
to brighten the darkness
with no comment
or judgment

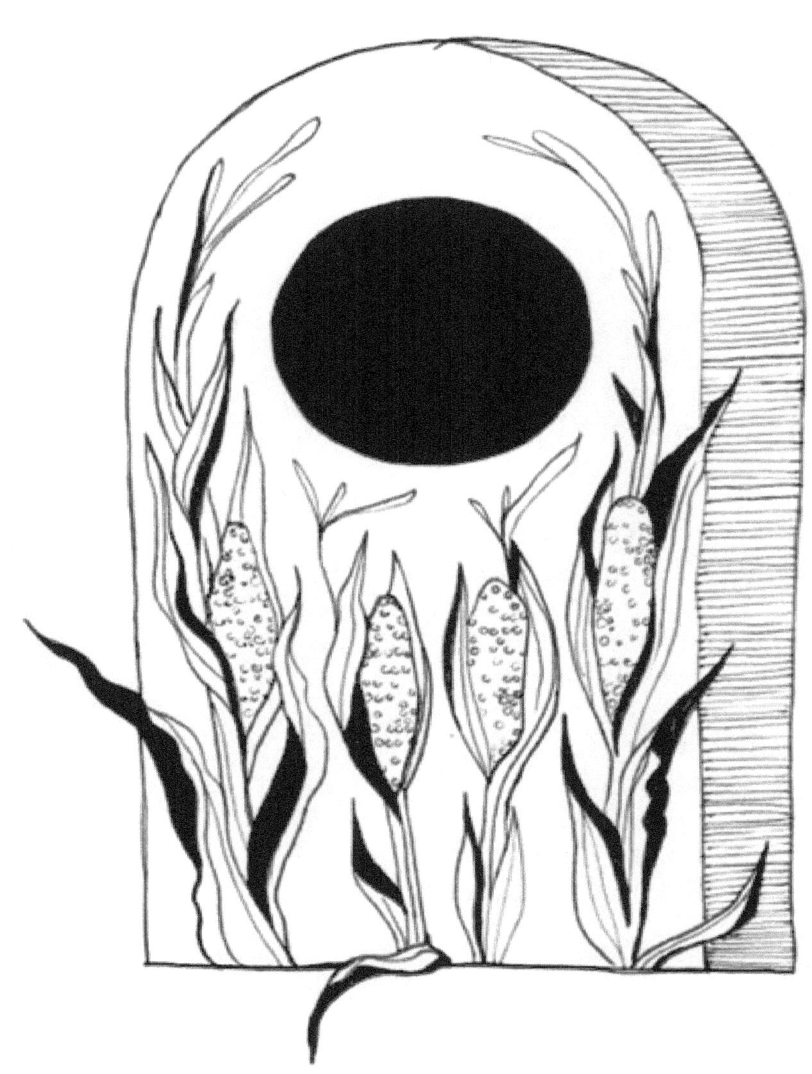

BLUE MOON

Once in a Blue Moon

On a cold night
winds whisk leaves from trees

a squirrel claws through mulch
searching for treasures

thick, dark clouds shroud the moon
while six trick-or-treaters

brave pandemic-filled streets
collecting sweet treats

Dad's candy delivery system
a ladder, PVC pipe and duct tape

deposits Nestle Crunch bars
into plastic bags or pumpkins

while adults watch from afar
always six feet apart

all await October's Blue Moon
and the presidential election

to bring light

NOVEMBER

Beaver Moon

Under November's full moon
when beavers build dams
no beavers swim in the pond
or slap their tails in alarm

But a great horned owl
almost hidden in the treetop
and some snowy egrets
nest for the night

As we wait for the moon
it explodes from behind
the mountains and rises as if
in a hurry to fully shine

The bright white moon
ripples in the pond
dancing on the water
twin moons, double moons

Then the drama dissipates
as the moon climbs higher
losing its mirrored image
and diminishes

Now it is simply
a full moon

DECEMBER

Winter Warmth

A full moon monopolizes
the dark, starry sky
temperatures plummet
as night claims daylight

December's Cold, Long Night Moon
Doesn't feel too long or cold
when her family gathers around a table
eating paella and drinking fine wine

After dinner her husband helps her clean the kitchen
so they can watch celebrity chefs create food art
whimsical, colorful, bursting-with-flavor masterpieces
then she crawls into bed under a pile of heavy blankets

She wakes when the sun rises late in the morning
reluctantly leaving her bedroom cocoon
to fix farmer's market eggs
while her husband lights a fire

As her favorite mug steams with green tea
she lounges on the sofa in her pajamas
reading and writing in front of hot,
popping, glowing embers

Despite daylight's arrival
the moon lingers
clear and
bright

EPILOGUE

After writing about each month's full moon, I find myself looking for the moon at other times. The moon mesmerizes me even when it's not full. I often notice it while I'm doing dishes. One night I wrote *Moon Grace* after struggling to make a nice dinner and dessert.

Moon Grace

The moon smiles down on me tonight
reminding me that God loves me

even if I don't make the best
eggplant parmesan

or if my chocolate
dipped orange slices
fail miserably

God in his infinite grace
smiles at me
for no other reason

than He loves
me

I've also noticed the moon from the car window. One morning my husband and I left for the airport at 6 AM. The moon stood over the mountain where the sun rises. The light from the sun was just beginning to appear. The dark silhouette of the Santa Catalina Mountains contrasted with a bright quarter moon in a lopsided smile, and the other three-quarters outlined in a shaded gray. Above the moon, candy-colored clouds completed the painting-worthy scene.

On another occasion, when I was leaving Green Bay, Wisconsin to return to Tucson, I sat in the back seat of my parent's car on our way to the airport. I looked up, and in the middle of the day, I saw an almost full moon. Above the moon, a cloud looked like an exclamation point, with the moon as the point. This haiku illustrates that moment:

> The moon punctuates
> an exclamation point
> made of clouds

As I marvel at the moon, I continue to ask questions to understand it better. Why does the moon look so big when it comes up? Why does the moon rise in different places at different times from one night to the next? The more I learn about the moon, the more awed I am, especially since the moon's light comes solely from the sun.

In the Bible's creation story found in the first chapter of Genesis, the moon is called "the lesser light" in comparison to the sun. Those words make me realize how much we have in common with the moon and perhaps why we are drawn to it.

the lesser light

not really its own light but the sun's reflection
we, like the moon, reflect God's radiance
not ours

all we have comes from Him
we're just dull gray landscape full of craters
no life within

petrified until God breathes
vitality into us
only then

do we begin to shine
when we mirror His
brilliance

Acknowledgements:

Special thanks to my critique group: Brad, David, Debra and Devi who continually encourage and challenge me in my writing. Thanks also to Karina for her valuable feedback and to my husband Chris for his generous support.

About the author:

Karen Admussen is a native Midwesterner transplanted into Arizona's Sonoran desert, where she is inspired by her surroundings. A former teacher and children's ministry director, Karen now writes poetry, memoir, and children's picture books. Several of her poems have been published in two Oro Valley Writers' Forum anthologies, *Monsoon Madness* and *Desert Muses.* Her next project is a chapbook of Sonoran Desert poems.

Karen can be contacted at karenadmussen@msn.com

About the illustrator:

Selena Harris is a Wisconsin-born artist based out of the beautiful Green Mountains of Vermont where she is currently studying Art Education. Multi-faceted in her love for the arts, Selena enjoys exploring a multitude of mediums including painting, illustrating, and sewing. Prior to her education at the University of Vermont, she worked in Ecuador as an English teacher and muralist, and is ecstatic to grow as an artist in the world of illustration and education.

Selena can be contacted either at sbharrisart@gmail.com or on Instagram @selenethebeann.